REVISED EDITION

Practical Pre-School

Planning for Learning through

People who help us

by Rachel Sparks Linfield and Christine Warwick Illustrated by Cathy Hughes

Contents

Published by Step Forward Publishing Limited

St Jude's Church, Dulwich Road, Herne Hill, London, SE24 0PB Tel. 020 7738 5454

Revised edition © Step Forward Publishing Limited 2008

First edition © Step Forward Publishing Limited 2000

www.practicalpreschool.com

All rights reserved. No part of this publication may be reproduced, stored in a retrieval system, or transmitted by any means, electronic, mechanical, photocopied or otherwise, without the prior permission of the publisher.

Planning for Learning through People who help us ISBN: 978 1 904575 53 5

Making plans

Why plan?

The purpose of planning is to make sure that all children enjoy a broad and balanced curriculum. All planning should be useful. Plans are working documents that you spend time preparing, but which should later repay your efforts. Try to be concise. This will help you in finding information quickly when you need it.

Long-term plans

Preparing a long-term plan, which maps out the curriculum during a year or even two, will help you to ensure that you are providing a variety of activities and are meeting the *Statutory Framework for the Early Years Foundation Stage* (2007).

Your long-term plan need not be detailed. Divide the time period over which you are planning into fairly equal sections, such as half terms. Choose a topic for each section. Young children benefit from making links between the new ideas they encounter so as you select each topic, think about the time of year in which you plan to do it. A topic about minibeasts will not be very successful in November!

Although each topic will address all the learning areas, some could focus on a specific area. For example, a topic on People Who Help Us would lend itself well to activities relating to Personal, Social and Emotional Development. Another topic might particularly encourage the appreciation of stories. Try to make sure that you provide a variety of topics in your long-term plans such as:

Autumn 1	Nursery rhymes
Autumn 2	Autumn / Christmas
Spring 1	People who help us
Spring 2	Colour
Summer 1	Clothes
Summer 2	Minibeasts

Medium-term plans

Medium-term plans will outline the contents of a topic in a little more detail. One way to start this process is by brainstorming on a large piece of paper. Work with your team writing down all the activities you can think of which are relevant to the topic. As you do this it may become clear that some activities go well together. Think about dividing them into themes. The topic of People Who Help Us, for example, has themes such as 'People who help us at home', 'People who help us to stay healthy', 'People who help to keep us safe' and 'People who help us to have food'.

At this stage, it is helpful to make a chart. Write the theme ideas down the side of the chart and put a different area of learning at the top of each column. Now you can insert your brainstormed ideas and will quickly see where there are gaps. As you complete the chart, take account of children's earlier experiences and provide opportunities for them to progress.

Refer back to the *Statutory Framework for the EYFS* and check that you have addressed as many different aspects of it as you can. Once all your medium-term plans are complete make sure that there are no neglected areas.

Making plans

Day-to-day plans

The plans you make for each day will outline aspects such as:

- resources needed;
- the way in which you might introduce activities;
- safety;
- the organisation of adult help;
- size of the group;
- individual needs;
- timing;
- key vocabulary.

Identify the learning and ELGs that each activity is intended to promote. Make a note of any assessments or observations that you are likely to carry out. On your plans make notes of which activities were particularly successful, or any changes you would make another time.

A final note

Planning should be seen as flexible. Not all groups meet every day, and not all children attend every day. Any part of the plan can be used independently, stretched over a longer period or condensed to meet the needs of any group. You will almost certainly adapt the activities as children respond to them in different ways and bring their own ideas, interests and enthusiasms. The important thing is to ensure that the children are

provided with a varied and enjoyable curriculum that meets their individual developing needs.

Using the book

- Collect or prepare suggested resources as listed on page 21.
- Read the section which outlines links to the Early Learning Goals (pages 4 - 7) and explains the rationale for the topic of People Who Help Us.
- For each weekly theme, two activities are described in detail as an example to help you in your planning and preparation. Key vocabulary, questions and learning opportunities are identified.
- The skills chart on page 23 will help you to see at a glance which aspects of children's development are being addressed as a focus each week.
- As children take part in the People Who Help Us topic activities, their learning will progress. 'Collecting evidence' on page 22 explains how you might monitor children's achievements.
- Find out on page 20 how the topic can be brought together in a grand finale involving parents, children and friends.
- There is additional material to support the working partnership of families and children in the form of a 'Home links' page, and a photocopiable 'Parent's page' found at the back of the book.

It is important to appreciate that the ideas presented in this book will only be a part of your planning. Many activities that will be taking place as routine in your group may not be mentioned. For example, it is assumed that sand, dough, water, puzzles, floor toys and large scale apparatus are part of the ongoing pre-school experience, as are the opportunities develop ICT skills. Role-play areas, stories, rhymes and singing, and group discussion times are similarly assumed to be happening each week although they may not be a focus for described activities. Groups should also ensure that there is a balance of adult-led and child-initiated activities.

The most enjoyable and memorable People Who Help Us topics for children involve visits from known adults who are willing to talk about the jobs that they do. It is vital, therefore, to plan early so that visitors may be invited and weekly themes can, if necessary, be postponed or brought forward.

Using the 'Early Learning Goals'

Having decided on your topic and made your medium-term plans you can use the *Statutory Framework for the Early Years Foundation Stage* to highlight the key learning opportunities your activities will address. The Early Learning Goals are split into six areas: Personal, Social and Emotional Development; Communication, Language and Literacy; Problem Solving, Reasoning and Numeracy; Knowledge and Understanding of the World; Physical Development and Creative Development. Do not expect each of your topics to cover every goal but your long-term plans should allow for all of them to be addressed by the time a child enters Year 1.

The following section lists the Early Learning Goals in point form to show what children are expected to be able to do by the time they enter Year 1 in each area of learning. These points will be used throughout this book to show how activities for a topic on People Who Help Us link to these expectations. For example, Personal, Social and Emotional Development point 7 is 'form good relationships with peers and adults'. Activities suggested which provide the opportunity for children to do this will have the reference PS7. This will enable you to see which parts of the Early Learning Goals are covered in a given week and plan for areas to be revisited and developed. In addition, you can ensure that activities offer variety in the goals to be encountered. Often a similar activity may be carried out to achieve different learning objectives. For example, during this topic children make houses from construction toys and fire-engine card ladders to rescue people from the roofs. Children will be

developing mathematical skills as they count and use the language of measurement to compare heights and lengths. In addition they will be developing aspects of technology as they build the homes and, also, personal and social skills as they talk and collaborate. It is important, therefore, that activities have clearly defined goals so that these may be emphasised during the activity and for recording purposes.

Personal, Social and Emotional Development (PS)

This area of learning covers important aspects of development that affect the way children learn, behave and relate to others.

By the end of the EYFS, children should:

PS1 Continue to be interested, excited and motivated to learn.

PS2 Be confident to try activities, initiate ideas and speak in a familiar group.

PS3 Maintain attention, concentrate and sit quietly when appropriate.

PS4 Respond to significant experiences, showing a range of feelings when appropriate.

PS5 Have a developing awareness of their own needs, views and feelings and be sensitive to the needs, views and feelings of others.

PS6 Have a developing respect for their own cultures and beliefs and those of other people.

PS7 Form good relationships with adults and peers.

PS8 Work as part of a group or class, taking turns and sharing fairly, understanding that there needs to be agreed values and codes of behaviour for groups of people, including adults and children, to work together harmoniously.

PS9 Understand what is right, what is wrong and why.

PS10 Consider the consequences of their words and actions for themselves and others.

PS11 Dress and undress independently and manage their own personal hygiene.

PS12 Select and use activities and resources independently

PS13 Understand that people have different needs, views, cultures and beliefs, that need to be treated with respect.

PS14 Understand that they can expect others to treat their needs, views, cultures and beliefs with respect.

The topic of People Who Help Us offers many opportunities for children's personal and social development. Time spent discussing the way people help them and considering the different jobs that people do will encourage children to speak in a group, to be interested and to consider consequences. By playing circle games children will learn to take turns and to understand the need for agreed codes of behaviour. Many of the areas outlined above, though, will be covered on an almost incidental basis as children carry out the activities described in this book for the other areas of children's learning. During undirected free choice times they will be developing PS12 whilst any small group activity that involves working with an adult will help children to work towards PS7.

Communication, Language and Literacy (L)

By the end of the EYFS, children should:

L1   Interact with others, negotiating plans and activities and taking turns in conversation.

L2   Enjoy listening to and using spoken and written language and readily turn to it in their play and learning.

L3   Sustain attentive listening, responding to what they have heard by relevant comments, questions or actions.

L4   Listen with enjoyment and respond to stories, songs and other music, rhymes and poems and make up their own stories, songs, rhymes and poems.

L5   Extend their vocabulary, exploring the meaning and sounds of new words.

L6   Speak clearly and audibly with confidence and control and show awareness of the listener, for example by their use of conventions such as greetings, 'please' and 'thank you'.

L7   Use language to imagine and recreate roles and experiences.

L8   Use talk to organise, sequence and clarify thinking, ideas, feelings and events.

L9   Hear and say sounds in words in the order in which they occur.

L10   Link sounds to letters, naming and sounding the letters of the alphabet.

L11   Use their phonic knowledge to write simple regular words and make phonetically plausible attempts at more complex words.

L12   Explore and experiment with sounds, words and texts.

L13   Retell narratives in the correct sequence, drawing on language patterns of stories.

L14   Read a range of familiar and common words and simple sentences independently.

L15   Know that print carries meaning and, in English, is read from left to right and top to bottom.

L16   Show an understanding of the elements of stories, such as main character, sequence of events, and openings and how information can be found in non-fiction texts to answer questions about where, who, why and how.

L17   Attempt writing for various purposes, using features of different forms such as lists, stories and instructions.

L18   Write their own names and other things such as labels and captions and begin to form simple sentences, sometimes using punctuation.

L19   Use a pencil and hold it effectively to form recognisable letters, most of which are correctly formed.

The activities suggested for the theme of People Who Help Us include several which are based on well-known picture books and stories. They allow children to enjoy listening to the books and to respond in a variety of ways to what they hear, reinforcing and extending their vocabularies. Throughout the topic opportunities are described in which children are encouraged to explore the sounds of words, to use descriptive vocabulary and to see some of their ideas recorded in both pictures and words. There are several activities that involve the making of both individual and group books. A number of role-play situations are described that will allow children to use their imaginations and to use speaking and writing within their play.

Problem Solving, Reasoning and Numeracy (N)

By the end of the EYFS, children should:

N1 Say and use number names in order in familiar contexts.
N2 Count reliably up to ten everyday objects.
N3 Recognise numerals one to nine.
N4 Use developing mathematical ideas and methods to solve practical problems.
N5 In practical activities and discussion begin to use the vocabulary involved in adding and subtracting.
N6 Use language such as 'more' or 'less' to compare two numbers.
N7 Find one more or one less than a number from one to ten.
N8 Begin to relate addition to combining two groups of objects and subtraction to 'taking away'.
N9 Use language such as 'greater', 'smaller', 'heavier' or 'lighter' to compare quantities.
N10 Talk about, recognise and recreate simple patterns.
N11 Use language such as 'circle' or 'bigger' to describe the shape and size of solids and flat shapes.
N12 Use everyday words to describe position.

The theme of People Who Help Us provides a meaningful context for problems solving, reasoning and numeracy. Children are given the opportunity to count milk bottles, measles, bricks and foods and to begin to develop language for addition and subtraction. There are opportunities for children to explore measurement, shape, size and position as they compare the lengths of fire-engine ladders, make biscuits and pretend to wash up. A number of counting games are suggested that use simple equipment and further reinforce the People Who Help Us theme.

Knowledge and Understanding of the World (K)

By the end of the EYFS, children should:

K1 Investigate objects and materials by using all of their senses as appropriate.
K2 Find out about, and identify, some features of living things, objects and events they observe.
K3 Look closely at similarities, differences, patterns and change.
K4 Ask questions about why things happen and how things work.
K5 Build and construct with a wide range of objects, selecting appropriate resources and adapting their work where necessary.
K6 Select the tools and techniques they need to shape, assemble and join materials they are using.
K7 Find out about and identify the uses of everyday technology and use information and communication technology and programmable toys to support their learning.
K8 Find out about past and present events in their own lives, and in those of their families and other people they know.
K9 Observe, find out about and identify features in the place they live and the natural world.
K10 Find out about their environment, and talk about those features they like and dislike.
K11 Begin to know about their own cultures and beliefs and those of other people.

The topic of People Who Help Us offers opportunities for children to make observations, to ask questions and to compare. They can investigate the time taken for dust to form and the best way to polish a window safely. By looking at pictures of old classrooms and talking to adults about the people who used to help them they will gain a sense of history. Activities such as making pelican crossing lights will help children to gain a greater understanding of the properties of materials.

Physical Development (PD)

By the end of the EYFS, children should:

PD1 Move with confidence, imagination and in safety.
PD2 Move with control and coordination.
PD3 Travel around, under, over and through balancing and climbing equipment.
PD4 Show awareness of space, of themselves and of others.
PD5 Recognise the importance of keeping healthy and those things which contribute to this.
PD6 Recognise the changes that happen to their bodies when they are active.

PD7   Use a range of small and large equipment.
PD8   Handle tools, objects, construction and malleable
      materials safely and with increasing control.

Activities such as playing with playdough and construction
toys will offer experience of PD8. Through playing 'The
keeper of the keys', 'Traffic lights' and pretending to do
the spring cleaning children will have the opportunity to
develop PD2. As children use large equipment and carry
out active games they will become more aware of how
their bodies change. Following physical activities children
are encouraged to consider how adults help them and
how they can help their peers and themselves.

Creative Development (C)

By the end of the EYFS, children should:

C1   Respond in a variety of ways to what they see, hear,
      smell, touch and feel.
C2   Express and communicate their ideas, thoughts
      and feelings by using a widening range of
      materials, suitable tools, imaginative and role play,
      movement, designing and making, and a variety of
      songs and musical instruments.
C3   Explore colour, texture, shape, form and space in
      two or three dimensions.
C4   Recognise and explore how sounds can be
      changed, sing simple songs from memory,
      recognise repeated sounds and sound patterns and
      match movements to music.
C5   Use their imagination in art and design, music,
      dance, imaginative and role play and stories.

During this topic children will experience working with
a variety of materials as they make spoon puppets, pasta
frames, models of bedrooms and print with sponges.
They will be able to develop their skills of painting
and colour mixing as they paint portraits and so work
towards C3. A number of songs that involve People Who
Help Us have been suggested which could have actions
and percussion added to allow children to use their
imaginations in music. Throughout all the activities
children are encouraged to talk about what they see and
feel, as they communicate their ideas in painting, music,
collage work and role play.

Week 1
People who help us at home

Personal, Social and Emotional Development

- Introduce the theme for the week and invite children to draw pictures of people who help them at home. Mount the pictures and display them on a board headed with the words 'This week we would like to thank these people for helping us'. In future weeks the display can be changed as different people are mentioned and the previous week's pictures made into a 'People who help us at/to...' class book. (PS2, 5)
- Discuss the different things that children can do to be helpful at home. Talk about cutlery and crockery, the safe way to carry them and how to set a table. Encourage children to take it in turns to role play being a parent and setting a table for their family. (PS8, 9)

Communication, Language and Literacy

- Help children to make individual 'People who help me at home' books in the shape of a house (see activity opposite). (L11, 18)
- Look at a picture of a person who delivers mail. Talk about the way they help people to keep in touch. Enjoy sharing *The Jolly Postman or Other People's Letters* by Janet and Allan Ahlberg (Heinemann) and looking at all the postcards and letters that the postman delivered. Provide a selection of envelopes and a variety of papers and cards for children to use for independent writing and role play. (L2, 4, 8)
- Help children to write labels for their pictures of people who help them at home. Use the labels to begin to make the class big book. (L18)

Problem Solving, Reasoning and Numeracy

- Talk about the way dishes are washed up at home. Encourage children to enjoy pretending to wash up a variety of containers in the water tray and to compare their sizes and the amounts of water that they can hold. (N9)
- Use sticky, regular shapes to make collages on paper plates of favourite foods that they eat at home. Encourage children to use shape vocabulary as they select shapes and to talk about their relative sizes. Invite children to help in displaying the plates and to talk about the people who make their meals at home and the things which children can do to help. (N11)

Knowledge and Understanding of the World

- Look at pictures of homes. Talk about all the jobs that have to be done to look after homes. Discuss the variety of cleaning, decorating and gardening tasks and the ways children might be able to help. Which jobs do children enjoy doing? (K8)
- Look at some pictures of homes with many windows. Talk about window cleaning and the way some people have window cleaners to look after their windows. As a group investigate the best way to polish a window. Ensure that the window is safe and then compare dry and wet cloths, and soap with no soap. Some people use newspapers to polish windows. Does it work? (K3, 4)
- Many people listen to or watch a weather forecast before they leave their homes every day. Discuss how helpful weather forecasters are and investigate different ways to forecast the weather including popular sayings. (K9)

Physical Development

- Play a game in which children are delivering bean-bag post. Encourage them to aim at a variety of high and low targets and to deliver their post quickly and safely. (PD1, 7)
- Tell a story in which a parent gets up and has a busy day ahead at home doing the spring cleaning. Encourage children to listen carefully to the tale and to mime and move in time with the words. (PD1, 2)

Creative Development

- Paint portraits of the people who help children at home. Use pasta to decorate the edge of large sheets of card. When dry, spray the pasta with gold or silver paint and use the pasta frames to display the portraits. (C3)
- Encourage children to enjoy playing in the home corner and to take on a variety of roles. Talk about how it feels to be a person helping at home. (C6)
- Make and decorate a bedroom from a cereal packet (see activity opposite). (C3)

Activity: Making 'People who help me at home' books

Learning opportunity: Making books and writing names.

Early Learning Goal: Communication, Language and Literacy. Children should write their own names and other things such as labels and captions... They will use their phonic knowledge to write simple regular words and make phonetically plausible attempts at more complex words.

Resources: Crayons; pencils; a picture book; for each child a book made from a piece of A4 card folded in half and cut in the shape of a house with a piece of A4 paper stapled inside.

Key vocabulary: Help, helpful, names of people, author, illustrator.

Organisation: Small group.

What to do: Remind children of the discussions about people who help them at home. Show them the house-shaped books and explain that they are each going to make a book about the people who help them at home. Show the children the pages and together count them. Ask children to say who they would like to draw in their books. Give each child a book and ask them to begin to draw one of the people they have suggested on the first page. Encourage them to put in details so that the person can be identified. At the same time either write the person's name on the page in a fluorescent pen for the child to overwrite, scribe or provide words to be copied.

When all four pages have been completed, decorate the covers with windows, a door and roof tiles. Show children a picture book, point out the author's and illustrator's names and explain that they are authors and illustrators. Encourage them to write their own names on their books.

Activity: Making cereal packet bedrooms

Learning opportunity: Making model bedrooms using a range of materials.

Early Learning Goal: Creative Development. Children should explore colour, texture, shape, form and space in two or three dimensions.

Resources: Small boxes, cotton reels, shells, cardboard tubes, carpet scraps, wallpaper, paper, fabric, paint; scissors; glue; cereal packets turned inside out with one large face removed.

Key vocabulary: Names for rooms in a house and bedroom furniture, wallpaper, carpet.

Organisation: Whole group, introduction, small group activity.

What to do: Remind children of the discussion they had about all the jobs that need to be done in a home. Talk about decorating rooms and the different ways this can be done. Who has wallpaper in their bedroom? Who has paint?

Show children a cereal packet that has been turned inside out and had one large face removed. Ask children to shut their eyes and to imagine that the box is their bedroom. What would they like to put in their room? How would they like to decorate it? Invite children to share their ideas and to look at samples of wallpapers.

Break up into smaller groups according to whether children wish to paint their room, to make wallpaper or use felt pens and crayons.

In follow-up sessions children could talk about floor covering and use scraps of carpet, fabric or paper to complete the decorating. Finally, furniture made from small boxes, cotton reels, shells or cardboard tubes and so on could be added.

Display

On a large noticeboard display the pictures of people who help children at home with the heading 'This week we would like to thank these people for helping us!' On a nearby table put out a book box of non-fiction books about people who help children. As the display is changed each week and big books are made with the pictures taken down, add the class books to the display.

On another board put up the cereal packet rooms in groups to form houses. Use corrugated card and textured papers to make roofs for the houses and ask children to suggest a name for the street.

Display the paper plates of food on a table covered with a tablecloth along with plastic play cutlery and beakers for children to practise setting tables.

Week 2

People who help us at school/nursery/pre-school

Personal, Social and Emotional Development

- During a circle time ask children to suggest the names of all the people who help them at school/ nursery/pre-school. Encourage them to think about the people who clean, who make meals, who look after the books, who set out activities and who answer the telephone. Talk about what would happen if one of the people was ill and could not do their work. Help the children to appreciate that each person has an important role. (PS2, 5)
- Ask children to paint or draw a portrait of someone who helps them at school/nursery/pre-school. Display these on the 'This week we would like to thank.....' noticeboard. (PS2, 5)
- Ask children to suggest ways that they could help those who help them. Talk about the importance of being tidy and putting toys away in their correct places. Demonstrate how to clean a table with a damp cloth and how to use a dustpan and brush. Throughout the week encourage children to be helpful and to think about how their actions affect others. (PS5, 8, 10)

Communication, Language and Literacy

- Turn the book corner into a library. Invite children to help to make tickets for books, labels for shelves/boxes and posters to show where different books are kept. Talk about the difference between non-fiction and fiction books. During the week encourage children to take it in turns to be a librarian and to run the group's library. (L2, 7, 17)
- Read *Mr Tick the Teacher* by Allan Ahlberg and Faith Jacques (Puffin Books). Is Mr Tick similar to teachers that the group know? Would children like to be taught by Mr Tick? All of Mr Tick's children's names begin with 't'. As a group make a word bank of names that begin with 't'. (L4, 9)
- Read a story about a child going to school for the first time such as *Billy and the Big New School* by Catherine and Laurence Anholt (Orchard Books) or 'In which Sophie Goes to School' in *Sophie's Tom* by Dick King-Smith (Walker Books). Talk about the reasons why the children were worried about going to school and the things that they looked forward to. What helped the children to be happy to go to school? (L4)

Problem Solvong, Reasoning and Numeracy

- Remind children of the discussion about putting toys away in their correct places. Provide children with baskets of shapes and ask them to help you to sort them. As children sort, encourage them to talk about the shapes, the number of edges/faces and their names. Ask children to make labels for the baskets and to count how many shapes are in each container. (N2, 11)
- Play the library game (see activity opposite). (N2, 3)

Knowledge and Understanding of the World

- Talk about the jobs that have to be done each day to keep the room clean. Investigate how long it takes for dust to form (see activity opposite). (K1, 3)
- Invite an adult known to the children to come and talk about their memories of school. Who were the people who helped them? What did they do to help their teachers and other adults? (K8)
- Help children to look closely at their surroundings and to notice how furniture is arranged and where things are kept. Encourage them to compare these observations with a picture of a classroom in the past with children seated in rows, writing on slates. Help them to notice people's expressions and to think about how it might have felt to be at school then. Who would have helped those schoolchildren? (K8, 10)

Physical Development

- Talk about the routines that are helpful when playing outside with large toys, such as stopping for a whistle or bell. Enjoy playing outside with large toys and encourage children to be helpful and also to appreciate how the adults that watch help them. (PD7)
- Talk about the rules that are necessary for using large apparatus safely. How do these rules help the teacher? How do the rules help children? Enjoy using large apparatus. Encourage children to understand both how they are helped and how they can help. (PD1)

Creative Development

- Help children to draw around one of their hands

and to cut it out. Decorate the hands with drawings of children or adults being helpful. Use the hands as leaves on a 'helping hand tree'. (C3)

- Set out the role-play area with a small blackboard and chalk; a variety of pens, crayons, pencils and papers; books and so on. Invite children to take it in turns to be the teacher and to enjoy helping their pupils. (C2)
- Make finger puppets from card circles of the people who help at school. Encourage children to enjoy using their puppets and to make up plays for their friends. (C5)

Activity: The library game

Learning opportunity: Counting to ten and recognising numerals to nine.

Early Learning Goal: Problem Solving, Reasoning and Numeracy. Children should count reliably up to ten everyday objects. They should recognise numerals 1 to 9.

Resources: Two sets of tickets with the numerals one to nine and four blank cards; 18 books with tickets (self-stick notes) with numerals one to nine.

Key vocabulary: Numbers one to nine, library, book, ticket.

Organisation: Small group.

What to do: Talk about the way librarians look after the books in a library and help people to borrow them. Show children the books and the numbers attached to each one. Explain that they are going to take it in turn to select a ticket and borrow the book which matches the ticket. Shuffle the number cards and put them number side down in the centre of the group. Invite children in turn to take a number card and match it to a book. (The blank card means miss a turn.) The game is finished when all the books have been borrowed. The winner is the person who has collected the most books.

Activity: Investigating dust

Learning opportunity: Observing and comparing.

Early Learning Goal: Knowledge and Understanding of the World. Children should investigate objects and materials by using all of their senses as appropriate. They should look closely at similarities, differences, patterns and change.

Resources: Duster; square of white card 10 x 10 cm; shelf or table which can remain untouched for up to a week.

Key vocabulary: Dust, clean.

Organisation: Whole group.

What to do: Talk about dust and the way it gathers in places. Clear a shelf or table and invite children to help to clean it with a damp duster. Tell them that although the furniture has been cleaned dust will come back. Invite the children to help you to find out how long it takes for dust to form. Explain that in order to do the experiment the furniture must not be touched or disturbed.

Lay the card square in the centre of the cleaned surface. Each morning, inspect the furniture with the children. When dust has appeared, remove the card square and help children to compare the clean, protected area with the dust-covered surface. Allow each child to run a finger over the dust to both see and feel it. Also, compare the dusty card with a clean piece. Finally, talk about the cleaning jobs which are carried out at school/nursery/pre-school and help children to appreciate why they take place at regular intervals.

Display

Cut out a large tree trunk and branches from brown sugar paper. Display it at floor height so that children feel it is a real tree. Stick the helping hands on the branches. Nearby put out a basket of extra paper hands and during the week encourage children to add more helping hands of things that they have noticed others doing to help them. Cut out a large 't' from paper. On this write all the 't' words that children suggested. Invite children to suggest more 't' words to fill the letter.

Practical Pre-School

Planning
for Learning
through
People who
help us

11

Week 3
People who help to keep us safe

Personal, Social and Emotional Development

- Invite a school crossing patrol person to talk to the group about their job and how to cross roads safely. (PS1, 2, 3, 7)
- Invite a person from the local fire station to come and talk to children about their job and how they help people. (Some stations may be willing to bring a fire engine to the group whilst others may run open days during the year.) (PS1, 2, 3, 7)
- During a circle time talk about safety and what children can do to help themselves. Encourage them to realise that although there are many people who help them to be safe they also have their parts to play. (PS9, 10)

Communication, Language and Literacy

- Talk about people who help children to cross the road safely and 'stop/go' signs. Provide card circles, straws and pens for children to make their own signs. Encourage them to write and read the words and use the signs in role-play. (L2, 6)
- Talk about sun safety and what parents and carers can do to help protect their children. Make sun saftety posters or leaflets. (L6, 19)

Problem Solving, Reasoning and Numeracy

- Ask children to make houses with windows from construction toys, to compare their heights and to make ladders to rescue play people (see activity opposite). (N9, 12)
- On a large sheet of paper draw a block of flats with six floors. On each floor draw two windows and put a play person in each window. Play a game in which children pretend to be a firefighter rescuing people. In order to rescue a person a die is thrown and a person is collected from the corresponding floor. As the game is played, encourage children to count the floors, the empty windows, the number of people rescued and how many more people need to be rescued to empty the building. (N1, 2, 6)

Knowledge and Understanding of the World

- Invite a police officer to talk to the group about the things that they do to help people to be safe. Record the visit with photographs. (K8)
- Show children a picture of a police officer directing traffic and one of people using lights to cross a road. Ask children to make lights to help people to cross a road (see activity opposite). (K5, 6)
- Examine a pushchair to look at safety straps. Talk about how they work. Provide boxes, ribbon, wool etc. for children to make safe pushchairs or chairs for a teddy. (K1, 5)
- Show children the safety warning on a toy which states that it is only suitable for children over the age of three years due to the presence of small parts which could be swallowed. Examine a selection of toys and sort them according to whether they would be safe for very young children. Some children may like to use cardboard tubes as a way to decide whether a toy or part is too small. Toys which can pass through the tube would be too tiny. Talk about the safety checks which toy factories would carry out to help to keep children safe. (K1, 2)

Physical Development

- Play the traffic light game in which colours indicate what children need to do. (Green means walk, amber means hop and red means stand absolutely still.) As you play the game, say the colours with different expression to encourage children to listen to what is said and not simply the way it is said. (PD1, 2, 4)
- Talk about how important it is to listen when you cross the road. Practise listening skills by playing 'The keeper of the keys'. A blindfolded child sits on a chair in the middle of a circle of children seated on the floor. Under the chair is a bunch of keys. In turn children try to tiptoe and take the keys. The keeper stops the keys being taken by pointing to where they hear a sound. Each keeper is allowed to point three times before another keeper is chosen. (PD2)

Creative Development

- Set out an area of the room as a town with roads, zebra and pelican crossings, fire, police and ambulance stations and a variety of play people and vehicles. Encourage children to enjoy playing in the town and to be people who help others to be safe. Provide signpost shapes cut from card, crayons and pencils and encourage children to make signs which could help people to be safe. (C5)

- Enjoy putting actions and percussion to songs and poems which feature people who help to keep us safe such as 'The fireman' in Apusskido Songs for Children, and 'London's Burning' (traditional). (C2)

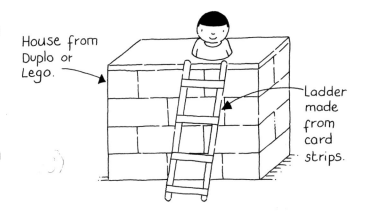

House from Duplo or Lego.

Ladder made from card strips.

Activity: Making fire-engine ladders

Learning opportunity: Comparing heights and talking about lengths and positions.

Early Learning Goal: Problem Solving, Reasoning and Numeracy. Children should use everyday words to describe position. They should use language such as 'greater', 'smaller', 'heavier' or 'lighter' to compare quantities.

Resources: Houses made from construction toys; strips of card; scissors; glue; toy fire engine with a ladder.

Key vocabulary: Taller, smaller, shorter, shortest, tallest, higher, lower, ladder, rescue.

Organisation: Small group.

What to do: Arrange the houses previously made from construction toys in a row and place a play person on each roof. Show children a toy fire engine with a ladder and talk about the way it can be used to rescue people from fires. Show children the street of houses and ask which one would need the longest ladder to rescue the person on the roof. As a group, arrange the houses in order of height. Finally, help children to make a ladder for each house from two strips of card with card rungs glued on. Throughout the work encourage children to compare lengths and heights and to describe where the people are positioned.

Activity: Making pelican crossing lights

Learning opportunity: Using a range of materials to construct pelican crossing lights.

Early Learning Goal: Knowledge and Understanding of the World. Children should build and construct with a wide range of objects, selecting appropriate resources and adapting their work where necessary. They should select the tools and techniques they need to shape, assemble and join the materials they are using.

Resources: Lolly sticks; cardboard tubes, straws; balsa wood; red and green cotton reels; red and green paper

and cellophane; plastic pots; Plasticine; glue; picture of people using a pelican crossing.

Key vocabulary: Red, green, pelican crossing, safe.

Organisation: Small group.

What to do: Talk to children about crossing the road. Where are the safest places to cross? Look at the picture of the pelican crossing and ask what the different lights mean. When can people cross the road? When must they not cross?

Invite children to make a pelican crossing. Show the group the resources. Ask the children to shut their eyes, to imagine what they are going to make and to raise a hand when they have an idea. Once all hands have been raised, ask them to explain what they are going to do. Encourage children to share ideas and to help friends to solve problems as they begin to carry out their constructing. When the lights have been finished, use them for play activities with toy cars and dolls.

Week 4
People who help us stay healthy

Personal, Social and Emotional Development

- During a circle time talk about how it feels to be unwell and the people who help to make us feel better. (Check beforehand that no child will be upset. Some family health problems could make this too sensitive an area for some children.) (PS1, 2, 3)
- Contact a local hospital or doctor's surgery and enquire whether they would like a frieze to decorate an area. As a group, talk about the importance of thanking those people who help to keep us healthy. Discuss what could go on the frieze and involve all children in making it. Once displayed, take a photo so that children can see where their work has gone. (PS5, 8)

Communication, Language and Literacy

- Sing 'Miss Polly had a dolly who was sick, sick, sick' from *Okki-tokki-unga Action Songs for Chidlren* chosen by Beatrice Harrop, Linda Friend and David Gadsby. Talk about how the dolly felt and who looked after her. Provide paper, crayons and pencils for the children to write bills for the doctor and to make 'Get Well' cards for the doll. (L11, 19)
- Tell the traditional tale of 'Jack and the Beanstalk'. Later in the week read to them the story of *Jim and the Beanstalk* by Raymond Briggs (Puffin) in which Jim helps the giant to have new teeth, glasses and a wig. Talk about the people who helped the giant to be healthier. (L3, 4)
- Involve children in making letter charts for a role-play optician's. Display the charts in a corner and invite children to take it in turns to be a customer or an optician. Encourage them to use the charts, talk on the telephone, make appointments in a diary and write customer reminders and bills for glasses. Provide a selection of plastic sun and play spectacles. (L2, 19)

Problem Solving, Reasoning and Numeracy

- Play the measles game (see activity opposite). (N2, 6)
- Use nine ambulances made from card and numbered from one to nine for number recognition and ordering activities. (N3)

Knowledge and Understanding of the World

- Invite a dentist to talk to the group about the way dentists help people to take care of their teeth and the importance of cleaning teeth. Talk about the way that sugary foods can harm them. Use a sand timer to demonstrate how long teeth should be brushed for each morning and evening. Ask children to make 'Clean your teeth!' posters. (K4)
- Ambulances which rush to emergencies have sirens and lights. Show children a picture of an ambulance and talk about the way the siren and light help people to know where ambulances are. Provide a range of percussion instruments and investigate which ones sound most like a siren. Which instruments would be most useful for warning people? (K2)
- Show children a selection of toy ambulances. Help them to make ambulances with moving wheels from boxes turned inside out, cotton reels, dowelling, plastic tubing and clothes pegs (see diagram opposite). (K2, 5)

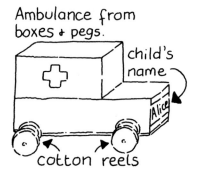

Ambulance from boxes & pegs.

child's name

cotton reels

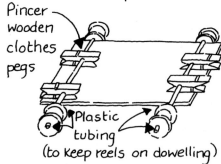

Underneath of ambulance.

Pincer wooden clothes pegs

Plastic tubing
(to keep reels on dowelling)

Physical Development

- Encourage children to move quickly and to enjoy running and jumping in a large space. Following the session, help children to notice the way their bodies change when they are active. Talk about the importance of taking exercise to be healthy. (PD5, 6)
- Talk to children about the way athletes and footballers often do circuit training to help to keep their bodies healthy. Make a simple circuit of activities such as walking along a bench, rolling a ball, jumping in and out of hoops and so on. Encourage children to use the circuit and to remember the instructions for each piece or set of equipment. (PD2, 4, 5)
- Play 'Simon says' in which all the actions are related to staying healthy such as peeling an apple, combing hair, washing hands, brushing teeth and going for a run. (PD1, 2, 4)

Creative Development

- Make a variety of hairstyles by trimming hair made from sugar paper attached to paper-plate faces (see activity opposite). (C3)
- Talk about people who take x-rays. Discuss how x-rays are used to show broken bones and how the bones can be set in plaster to help them mend. Read Funnybones by Janet and Allan Ahlberg (Picture Lions). Make x-rays from white card bones on thin black or grey paper. (C3)
- Make dolls from wooden spoons with two faces, one that is sad and unwell and one that is happy and healthy. Encourage children to use their dolls whilst singing 'Miss Polly had a dolly who was sick, sick, sick'. (C2)

Activity: The measles game

Learning opportunity: Counting to ten and comparing numbers.

Early Learning Goal: Problem Solving, Reasoning and Numeracy. Children should count reliably up to ten everyday objects. They should use language such as 'more' or 'less' to compare two numbers.

Resources: Red counters; faces drawn on large paper plates; a die numbered one to six; a box lined with felt in which to throw the die.

Key vocabulary: Spot, measles, numbers one to ten, more, fewer, fewest, most.

Organisation: Small group.

What to do: Give each child a paper face and ten counters. Ask them to check how many counters they have and to lay them out on their plate face. Explain that the people have measles and they are going to be the nurses who help to make them better. Invite children to take it in turn to roll the die and to remove the number of spots indicated. After each go encourage children to say how many spots they had, how many they have taken away and the number that are left. The game finishes when no spots remain.

Activity: Cutting paper hair

Learning opportunity: Using scissors.

Early Learning Goal: Creative Development. Children should explore colour, shape, form and space in two or three dimensions.

Resources: For each child a paper plate with long strips of sugar paper firmly stapled on as hair to be trimmed; scissors; felt pens.

Key vocabulary: Hair, long, short, curly, straight, hairdresser, cut, trim.

Organisation: Small group.

What to do: Remind children of the importance of looking after their hair and the way that people who trim and wash our hair help us to do this. Provide each child with a paper-plate head with hair made from long strips of sugar paper. Ask children to pretend that they are hairdressers and to trim the hair on the paper-plate heads. Remind children that once cut the hair cannot be glued back on! Show children how by wrapping the paper around their fingers firmly the hair can be helped to wave. To finish, give each head a face. Remind children where to position eyes.

Note: Because paper plates tend to have a waxy surface, this activity works best if the back of the plate is used as the face.

Display

Make a sign that says 'For healthy hair come to ....'s hair salon'. Use border paper to create a shop window effect. Arrange the group's paper hairstyles in the 'window'. Use the town layout made the previous week to display the box ambulances. On a nearby table put out the measles game and the card ambulances for children to play with during free play. Stick the x-rays on windows, if possible, along with a real x-ray. Nearby put out a plastic model skeleton or poster of one.

Week 5
People who help us to have food

Personal, Social and Emotional Development

- Show children the ingredients for a cake or biscuits. Talk about where they came from and help children to realise that many stages come before a product is sold in a shop. (PS1, 2, 8)
- Invite a shopkeeper, milk delivery person, gardener, farmer, baker and/or cook to talk about how they help people to have food and what they do. Before the visits discuss with children the types of questions that they might ask. (PS1, 2, 7, 8)

Communication, Language and Literacy

- Make posters to advertise foods on sale in a role-play shop. (L4, 17, 19)
- Read *Oliver's Fruit Salad* or/and *Oliver's Vegetables* by Vivian French (Hodder Children's Books). Make concertina flap books of favourite fruits or vegetables (see activity opposite). (L3, 9, 19)
- Use pictures of foods for matching to their initial sounds and for playing 'Find the food which is delivered by/sold by/comes from...'. (L2, 9)

Problem Solving, Reasoning and Numeracy

- Use the 'Milk van' counting rhyme (see activity opposite). (N1, 7)
- Use the favourite food concertina flap books for counting activities. (N1, 2)
- Set out the role-play area as a grocery store with posters, price lists, a toy cash register, play foods, paper bags, plastic baskets and money. Encourage children to enjoy buying and selling food. (N3, 5)
- Make shortbread biscuits with plastic cutters. (Check first for children's food allergies and area health and safety guidelines for cooking activities.) As children help, encourage them to compare quantities of ingredients, to count the biscuits and to talk about the shapes of the biscuits they make. (N2, 4, 11)

Knowledge and Understanding of the World

- Look at the pictures of the fruits in *Oliver's Fruit Salad* by Vivian French (Hodder Children's Books). Investigate which fruits can be grown from pips. Encourage children to collect pips from fruit they eat at home and plant them. (K2, 3)

- Enjoy looking at the pictures in a book about farming such as *1001 Things to Spot on the Farm* by Gillian Doherty (Usborne). Help children to notice all the things which farmers have to do to grow crops and look after animals. Encourage children to ask questions and to enjoy discovering facts about the way farmers help to provide food. (K4)

Physical Development

- Observe a range of fruits and make fruits from playdough. (PD8)
- Use skittles as milk bottles for races. Set out skittles in rows and ask children to collect the 'empty bottles'. Carry out simple relays in which a skittle is 'delivered'. (PD2)

Creative Development

- Make a large patchwork of clean food labels. During the week ask children to collect labels from all the foods that they eat and to stick them on to a large noticeboard so that all spaces are filled. Encourage children to think about the shape and colour of each label and where it would look best in the patchwork. (C3)
- Use sponges cut in the shape of fruits and vegetables or firm fruits and vegetables and ready-mixed paint for printing. The prints are especially effective if done on black sugar paper. (C3)
- Look at pictures of food markets. Look at the types of foods that are sold and how they are arranged on the stalls. Invite children to paint large portraits of

people buying or selling food to go on a group frieze of a market. Also involve children in the painting of fruits and vegetables to cut out for the stalls. (C3)

Activity: Making concertina flap books

Learning opportunity: Making books and writing initial sounds.

Early Learning Goal: Communication, Language and Literacy. Children should sustain attentive listening, responding to what they have heard by relevant comments, questions or actions. They should use a pencil and hold it effectively to form recognisable letters, most of which are correctly formed. They should hear and say sounds in the order in which they occur.

Resources: Copies of *Oliver's Fruit Salad* or/and *Oliver's Vegetables* by Vivian French (Hodder Children's Books); for each child a concertina flap book made from a folded sheet of A4 sized card (see diagram); pencils; crayon.

Key vocabulary: Book, page, author, names of fruits and vegetables, author, illustrator.

Organisation: Small group.

What to do: On a previous day read either or both the Oliver books. Before introducing the concertina books talk about fruits and vegetables that children like and why they taste special. Look at the pictures in the Oliver books and encourage the children to consider why Oliver did not initially like certain foods and how his grandparents helped him to like them.

Show children the concertina books and explain that they are each going to make a book about their favourite vegetables or fruits. Show how to lift the flaps and explain that the food will be drawn under the flap. Ask children to tell you what they would like to draw and check that they are aware of the shapes and colours of the fruits and vegetables.

When all drawings and colouring has been completed help the children to write the initial letter for each fruit

and vegetable on the flaps, and the word underneath. Remind the children that they are the authors and illustrators and their names should be on their books. Later in the week use the books to play 'I spy a fruit/vegetable under the flap that begins with ......'

Activity: The milk van counting rhyme

Learning opportunity: Counting to ten.

Early Learning Goal: Problem Solving, Reasoning and Numeracy. Children should say and use number names in order in familiar contexts. They should find one more or one less than a number from one to ten.

Resources: None.

Key vocabulary: Numbers ten to zero, crate, milk, bottle, van.

Organisation: Whole group.

What to do: Recite the following rhyme to the group, showing the actions and encouraging children to join in with the counting. As the rhyme progresses children are likely to join in with the words and the actions.

I met a milk van	(with arms mime wheels)
With <u>ten</u> cartons in a crate.	(show ten fingers)
I bought <u>one</u> carton	(put down one finger)
The milk tasted great!	(mime drinking milk)
That left <u>nine</u> cartons	(Show and count
on the van.	nine fingers)

Later in the day repeat the rhyme but with children taking a greater part in the reciting and counting. On further occasions the rhyme could include a child with ten washed-out milk cartons or skittles to deliver; throw a die numbered from nought to two to govern how many cartons can be bought each time.

Display

Involve children in displaying their food labels to make the large patchwork and in providing the background for the market frieze. Use large brushes or sponges to paint the sky and ground for the market. Make stalls from cardboard boxes and place these in front of the board. Invite children to position their market traders and shoppers and to help in arranging the painted fruits and vegetables on the stalls. Mount the fruit and vegetable prints on brightly coloured paper and combine them to make a second large patchwork. Use the patchworks for counting activities. In a nearby basket place the concertina flap books.

Week 6
The thank you party

Personal, Social and Emotional Development

- Explain to the children that there is going to be a party to say thank you to all the people that they have been thinking about over the past few weeks. Talk about the preparations needed. (PS3, 8)
- Use the big books that children have made as the stimulus for making a list of people that children would like to invite to the thank you party. (PS3, 7)
- During a circle time encourage children to complete the sentence 'I want to thank .... because.....................'. (PS3, 8)

Communication, Language and Literacy

- Involve children in the making of invitations for the party. Help them to fill in the name of the person being invited and the group's name. (L19)
- Read *Alfie and the Birthday Surprise* by Shirley Hughes (The Bodley Head). Ask children why the surprise party was planned and how it helped to cheer up Bob MacNally. Talk about the preparations that took place for the party and the ones the children will need to make for their thank-you party. (L4)
- As a group, make up a story about some of the people who have visited during the topic. Scribe the tale on large pieces of paper and make it into a big book illustrated by the children. Show children some picture books which have dedications. Explain what a dedication is and dedicate the group's book to the people who help them. (L4)

Problem Solving, Reasoning and Numeracy

- Use the party as the stimulus for counting activities. Count the number of people who are invited, the number of people who say they can come, the number of thank you certificates that need to be made, and so on. (N1, 2)
- Enjoy replaying games used within the People Who Help Us topic. Invite children to choose their favourite games and also to think about how the rules could be altered to make a new game. (N - depends on the games chosen)
- Involve children in making a number frieze of pictures associated with the people that are to be thanked. For instance, the frieze could be of one nurse, two farmers, three nurses and so on, or it might be of objects such as one fire engine, two milk cartons, three envelopes, four rubbish sacks and so on. Encourage children to suggest ideas for the number frieze. (N1, 2, 3)

Knowledge and Understanding of the World

- On a computer make thank you certificates. Involve children in selecting the font, colour and decoration. Talk about the way that the computer is useful for producing a large number of certificates quickly and the ease with which text and pictures can be altered. (K7)
- Make shakers from rice and plastic tubs to accompany the thank you song (see Creative Development). (K1)
- Show children pictures of a variety of parties such as street parties, birthday parties and so on. Talk about the occasions for which parties are held including ones from a range of cultures. (K11)

Physical Development

- Play the thank you ball-rolling game (see activity opposite). (PD7)
- Encourage children to travel around, under, over and through balancing and climbing equipment in the role of a helping person who has been mentioned during the topic. Examples could include a milk delivery person who stops at each piece of equipment to leave milk, a market stall holder who carries imaginary boxes, a police officer who moves quickly and safely between equipment and a lighthouse keeper who climbs to put the light on. (PD1, 2, 3)
- Play 'The farmer's in his den' (traditional) but change the words to include the people who children have been thinking about (for example 'The teacher's in her school; The doctor's in her surgery; The driver's in his bus'). Encourage children to move in time with the words and to invent actions for each of the characters. (PD1)

Creative Development

- Practise the 'Thanking day song' (see activity right). (C4)
- Write each of the letters in 'thank you' on large

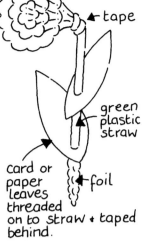

sheets of card or stiff paper. Divide the children into small groups and give a letter to each one. Encourage the children to decorate their letters. Use them to make a thank you banner. (C3)

- Use tissue-paper circles, green plastic straws, clear tape, green paper leaves and silver foil to make thank you button holes (see diagram above). (C3)

Activity: The thank you ball-rolling game

Learning opportunity: Rolling balls and playing a collaborative game.

Early Learning Goal: Physical Development. Children should use a range of small equipment.

Resources: A variety of large and small plastic and sponge balls.

Key vocabulary: Names of people in the group, roll, ball, thank you.

Organisation: Whole group sitting on the floor in a circle.

What to do: Demonstrate to the group how a ball can be rolled across the circle. Show children how to aim the ball and how to push it hard enough to reach someone but not so hard that it goes out of the circle. Once all children have had the chance to practise rolling a ball, ask them to stand up, still in the circle. Explain that they are each going to have a turn at rolling the ball. Before sending the ball they must say 'I'm going to send the ball to ....'. After they have rolled the ball they should sit down. Try the activity several times, encouraging children to keep an eye on the ball, to send it quickly and to sit quietly.

Challenge the children to complete the circle rolling before you have counted to a certain number or before the sand has gone through a sand timer. On other occasions repeat the activity and as well as naming the person who is to receive the ball ask children to say 'Thank you .... for ....'

Before starting, talk about the sorts of things children might wish to say thank you for. Changing the size of the ball can add further variety.

Activity: The thanking day song

Learning opportunity: Singing and playing percussion instruments.

Early Learning Goal: Creative Development. Children should recognise and explore how sounds can be changed, (and) sing simple songs from memory...

Resources: Shakers.

Key vocabulary: Words for the song, loud, louder, soft, quietly.

Organisation: Whole group sitting on the floor.

What to do: To the tune of 'Happy birthday to you' sing the 'Thanking day' song.

Happy thanking day to you,

Happy thanking day to you,

We want to say thank you

For all that you do!

Explain to the children that this song will be sung at the thank you party for all the people the children want to thank. Teach the words of the song to the group. Show children how the speed can be changed and the volume. Say that the song should sound happy and ask children to suggest how it should be sung. Hand out the shakers and let children experiment with the ways that they can be played. Finally, sing the song once without shakers and once with them to produce a grand finale.

Display

Hang the thank you banner in a prominent position to welcome people to the party. Check displays for loose corners and pieces which may have come adrift. Set out all the books that have been made during the topic. Line baskets with green crepe paper and arrange the button holes ready to present to people at the thank you party.

Bringing It All Together

The thank you party

Before starting the People Who Help Us topic, alert those who will be invited to the party of the date and ask whether they are likely to be able to attend. In this way, planning can take place for approximate numbers and children will be saved from too many rejections!

Preparation

Explain to children that the purpose of the party is to say thank you to their families, friends and people who have visited during the topic. Talk about how it feels to be thanked and ask for suggestions for the kinds of things that might happen at the party.

With the children plan and practise a small presentation in which they can show something that has been made during the topic, recite rhymes and sing songs.

Allocate jobs so that all children have something special to do. This might be presenting the button holes and certificates, handing around food or welcoming people with an adult.

Food

No party is complete without food but the type and amount is likely to depend on the number of people expected to attend. Possible foods include:

- slices of apple dunked in melted chocolate
- egg baskets made from cornflakes, melted chocolate and mini chocolate eggs
- savoury biscuits
- gingerbread people iced as police, nurses and so on
- drink made from a mixture of fruit juices and lemonade

For an extra special party feeling straws could be decorated by children using small pieces of card with two slits for the straw to slip through (see diagram).

The party

Start the party with the presentation by the children. Ensure that items by individual children are balanced with ones by the whole group. Doing this reduces the urge to fidget! Involve all children in reciting rhymes used during the project, singing the 'Happy thanking day' song and playing their shakers. Finally, invite children to give to each person present their thank you certificate and paper flower button-hole.

Following the presentation, ask people to remain seated whilst children, with adults to supervise, hand round the food and drinks. To finish invite the guests to look around the displays and to participate in a quiz. Prepare, on one side of A4 paper, 20 simple questions for an adult to complete with a child. Include questions to do with the presentation, the food and the displays. Provide each pair with the quiz and a pencil and give small prizes for completed quizzes.

Resources

All books were available from leading booksellers at the time of writing

Resources to collect

- Dressing-up clothes for police, nurses, cooks and so on.
- Toys for role-play shops, cafes, market stalls, opticians and so on.
- Poster or plastic model of a human skeleton.
- An x-ray or picture of an x-ray of a human bone.
- Wooden spoons.

Everyday resources

- Boxes, large and small, for modelling.
- Papers and cards of different weights, colours and textures, for example sugar paper, tissue-paper circles, corrugated card, silver and shiny papers.
- Dry powder paints for mixing and mixed paints for covering large areas.
- Different sized paint brushes from household brushes to thin brushes for delicate work and a variety of paint mixing containers.
- A variety of drawing and colouring pencils, crayons, pastels, charcoals and so on.
- Additional decorative and finishing materials such as sequins, foils, glitter, tinsel, shiny wool and threads, beads, pieces of textiles, parcel ribbon.
- Table covers; pasta; green plastic straws; plastic cotton reels; cereal packets; paper plates.

Stories

- *Funnybones* by Janet and Allan Ahlberg (Puffin Books).
- *Mr Tick the Teacher* by Allan Ahlberg and Faith Jacques (Puffin Books).
- *The Jolly Postman* or *Other People's Letters* by Janet and Allan Ahlberg (Heinemann).
- *The Jolly Pocket Postman* by Janet and Allan Ahlberg (Heinemann).
- *Billy and the Big New School* by Catherine and Laurence Anholt (Orchard Books).
- *Jim and the Beanstalk* by Raymond Briggs (Puffin).
- *Oliver's Fruit Salad* by Vivian French (Hodder Children's Books).
- *Oliver's Vegetables* by Vivian French (Hodder Children's Books).
- *Alfie and the Birthday Surprise* by Shirley Hughes (Red Fox).
- *An Evening At Alfie's* by Shirley Hughes (Red Fox).
- *Sophie's Tom* by Dick King-Smith (Walker Books).

Non-fiction

- *1001 Things to Spot on the Farm* by Gillian Doherty (Usborne).

Songs

- *Okki-tokki-unga Action Songs for Children* chosen by Beatrice Harrop, Linda Friend and David Gadsby (A & C Black).
- *Apusskido Songs for Children* chosen by Beatrice Harrop, Peggy Blakely and David Gadsby (A & C Black).

Information for Adults

- *The Early Years Foundation Stage Setting the Standards for Learning, Development and Care for Children from birth to five* - Department of Education and Skills

Collecting Evidence of Children's Learning

Monitoring children's development is an important task. Keeping a record of children's achievements, interests and learning styles will help you to see progress and will draw attention to those who are having difficulties for some reason. If a child needs additional professional help, such as speech therapy, your records will provide valuable evidence.

Records should be the result of collaboration between group leaders, parents and carers. Parents should be made aware of your record keeping policies when their child joins your group. Show them the type of records you are keeping and make sure they understand that they have an opportunity to contribute. As a general rule, your records should form an open document. Any parent should have access to records relating to his or her child. Take regular opportunities to talk to parents about children's progress. If you have formal discussions regarding children about whom you have particular concerns, a dated record of the main points should be kept.

Keeping it manageable

Records should be helpful in informing group leaders, adult helpers and parents and always be for the benefit of the child. The golden rule is to make them simple, manageable and useful.

Observations will basically fall into three categories:

- **Spontaneous records:** Sometimes you will want to make a note of observations as they happen, for example, a child is heard counting cars accurately during a play activity, or is seen to play collaboratively for the first time.

- **Planned observations:** Sometimes you will plan to make observations of children's developing skills in their everyday activities. Using the learning opportunity identified for an activity will help you to make appropriate judgements about children's capabilities and to record them systematically.

To collect information:
- talk to children about their activities and listen to their responses;
- listen to children talking to each other;
- observe children's work such as early writing, drawings, paintings and 3D models. (Keeping photocopies or photographs is useful.)

Sometimes you may wish to set up 'one off' activities for the purposes of monitoring development. Some pre-school groups, for example, ask children to make a drawing of themselves at the beginning of each term to record their progressing skills in both co-ordination and observation. Do not attempt to make records after every activity!

- **Reflective observations:** It is useful to spend regular time reflecting on the children's progress. Aim to make some brief comments about each child every week.

Informing your planning

Collecting evidence about children's progress is time consuming and it is important that it is useful. When you are planning, use the information you have collected to help you to decide what learning opportunities you need to provide next for children. For example, a child who has poor pencil or brush control will benefit from more play with dough or construction toys to build the strength of hand muscles.

Example of recording chart

Name: Jonathan Hogg		D.O.B. 18.2.04			Date of entry: 13.9.08
Term	**Personal, Social and Emotional Development**	**Communication, Language and Literacy**	**Problem Solving, Reasoning and Numeracy**	**Knowledge and Understanding of the World**	**Physical Development**	**Creative Development**
ONE	Reluctant to say goodbye to mother. Prefers adult company. Loved talking to the fireman and asked sensitive questions. 20.9.08 EMH	Enjoys listening to stories, particularly enjoyed the 'Alfie' stories. Can write first name. Good pencil grip. 20.11.08 EMH	Is able to say numbers to ten and count accurately five objects. Recognises and names sqaures and circles. 5.11.08 EHL	Very eager to ask questions. Is fascinated by the computer and always eager to have a turn. 16.10.08 LSS	Can balance on one leg. Does not like the feel of playdough. Particularly ken to use climbing equipment 16.10.08 APW	Enjoys painting and particularly when mixing own colours. His portraits show good observation and memory for details. Does not find it easy to use scissors 20.10.08 EMH
TWO						
THREE						

Planning for Learning through People who help us

Skills overview of six-week plan

Week	Topic Focus	Personal, Social and Emotional Development	Communication, Language and Literacy	Problem Solving, Reasoning and Numeracy	Knowledge and Understanding of the World	Physical Development	Creative Development
1	People who help us at home	Listening; Expressing emotions; Role-play	Listening to stories; Writing	Recognising numbers; Capacity; Recognition of 2-D shapes; Counting	Making observations; Comparing; Investigating; Talking	Moving with control and imagination; Using construction toys	Role-play; Collage; Painting
2	People who help us at school	Listening; Taking turns; Sensitivity to others; Developing independence	Listening to stories; Listening; Writing; Hearing and saying sounds	Counting; Comparative language; Recognition of shapes	Making observations; Comparing; Describing; Investigating; Talking	Moving with control safety, with awareness of space and imagination; Using large equipment	Drawing; Role-play; Making finger puppets
3	People who help to keep us safe	Considering actions; Safety awarness; Listening	Speaking; Writing; Role-play	Comparative language; Counting; Recognising numbers; Making repeating pattens	Talking; Constructing; Designing	Moving with control and imagination; Balancing	Singing; Painting; Role-play
4	People who help us to stay healthy	Discussing emotions; Sensitivity to others; Speaking; Listening	Listening to stories; Responding to stories; Writing	Comparative language; Counting; Recognising numbers	Talking; Observing; Investigating; Constructing	Moving with control and imagination;	Using materials; Cutting; Singing; Making spoon dolls
5	People who help us to have food	Taking turns; Listening; Speaking	Listening to a story; Writing a purpose; Hearing and saying sounds; Discussing	Counting; Recognising shapes; Comparative language	Investigating; Observing; Talking	Moving with control; Aiming; Using malleable materials	Printing; Collage; Painting
6	The thank you party	Expressing emotions; Collaborative planning	Listening to a story; Writing for a purpose; Making up a story	Recognising numbers; Counting	Using ICT; Investigating; Comparing	Moving with control and imagination and awarness of space; Aiming	Collage; Using materials; Singing

Home links

The theme of People Who Help Us lends itself to useful links with children's homes and families. Through working together children and adults gain respect for each other and build comfortable and confident relationships.

Establishing partnerships

- Keep parents informed about the topic of People Who Help Us, the themes for each week and the proposed date for the thank-you party. By understanding the work of the group, parents will enjoy the involvement of contributing ideas, time and resources.
- Photocopy the parent's page for each child to take home.
- Invite friends, childminders and families to join in the thank-you party .

Visiting enthusiasts

- Invite adults to come to the group to talk about how they help people. Remember to include a range of professions, people who work in the home and those who children see each day. Ensure that the visitors are well briefed so that children are enthused.